비 해피 영어회화

비 해피 영어회화

Be Happy English Conversation

초등학생 영어회화

최종수 엮음

YMS미디어

머리말

영어회화의 기본 목표는 의사소통과 이해입니다. 한국 사람인 나와 영어를 사용하는 상대방 사이에서 오가는 말을 서로 충분히 알아듣고 이해해야 한다는 것입니다. 여기에서 중요한 것은 말을 짧게, 쉽게, 그리고 정확하게 하는 것입니다. 그래야만 말하고자 하는 것이 틀리지 않고 분명하게 전달되기 때문입니다. 이 책에서 보여준 예문들은 모두 그러한 목적에 맞는 말들입니다.

이 책에는 약 300개의 짧은 말들이 있습니다. 그 대부분이 영어 원어민들이 일상생활에서 아주 흔히 쓰는 말들입니다. 생각을 해서 말하기보다는 입에서 저절로 나오는 말들입니다. 한국 사람이 이런 말을 잘하면 그들에게는 영어가 상당히 유창하고 세련되게 들립니다.

영어회화를 잘 하기 위해서는 엄청나게 많은 시간과 노력이 필요한 것은 아닙니다. 이 책으로 하루에 10~20분 정도 꾸준히 두 달만 공부하면 됩니다. 그 동안 자연스레 영어에 대한 감각을 익히게 되고, 마침내 영어회화가 가능해집니다. 영어에 확신을 가지게 되고, 원어민이 놀랄 만큼의 영어 실력과 회화 능력을 갖추게 되는 것입니다. 그 다음의 영어 학습은 해석과 작문입니다.

이 책을 보는 모든 학생들은 자신감과 희망을 가지고 공부를 시작하기 바랍니다. 그리고 이 책을 마칠 때쯤 되면 이미 영어회화, 나아가 영어라는 하나의 언어가 자신의 생각과 생활 속에 스며들어 있음을 알게 됩니다.

2005년 여름에 최종수

차례

일러두기

이 책은 한 학생의 1주일 동안의 생활을 가상하여 꾸며졌습니다.
1주일 7일 동안에 하루 7항목씩 모두 49개의 항목이 있습니다.
이 49개의 항목을 49일 동안 공부하고 테스트를 하루 치러 모두 50일 동안
공부하도록 되어 있습니다.
한 항목은 두 페이지씩으로 되어 있습니다. 한 페이지에는 회화 문장이 있고
다른 한 페이지는 쓰면서 익히도록 되어 있습니다.
테스트는 한 문제에 5점씩 100점 만점으로 계산하여 80점 이상 되어야 합니다.
답이 틀린 문제는 다시 한번 공부하여 확실히 익히도록 합니다.

이 책을 공부할 때는 이렇게 해야 합니다.

❶ 하루에 두 페이지씩 공부합니다.
　　먼저 왼쪽 페이지를 읽고 다음에 오른쪽 페이지의 쓰기를 합니다.
❷ 공부하는 날의 날짜를 오른쪽 위에 적습니다.
❸ 쓰기를 할 때는 큰소리로 읽으면서 씁니다.
❹ 희미한 글씨 위에 한 번 덧쓰고 그 아래 밑줄 위에 계속 씁니다.

제 1 일

1. 기상

Wake up!	일어나라!
I'm sleepy.	졸려요.
It's time to get up.	일어날 시간이야.
Just five minutes more, please.	5분만 더요, 제발.
You are late.	늦었어.
That's too bad.	너무 해.

Wake up!

Wake up!　　　　　　　　　　　　Wake up!

I'm sleepy.

I'm sleepy.　　　　　　　　　　　I'm sleepy.

It's time to get up.

It's time to get up.　　　　　　　It's time to get up.

Just five minutes more, please.

Just five minutes more, please.　Just five minutes more, please.

You are late.

You are late.　　　　　　　　　　You are late.

That's too bad.

That's too bad.　　　　　　　　　That's too bad.

2. 등교

Hi!	안녕!
Peek-a-Boo!	까꿍!
What are you doing?	뭐하고 있어?
I'm preparing the class.	수업 준비하고 있지.
You are kidding.	농담하고 있네.
I'm serious.	진짜야.

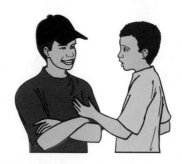

Hi!

Hi!

Hi!

Peek-a-Boo!

Peek-a-Boo!

Peek-a-Boo!

What are you doing?

What are you doing?

What are you doing?

I'm preparing the class.

I'm preparing the class.

I'm preparing the class.

You are kidding.

You are kidding.

You are kidding.

I'm serious.

I'm serious.

I'm serious.

3. 친구

Did you finish your homework? 숙제 다 해 왔니?

Oops, I forgot it. 아이쿠, 깜빡 잊었네.

Are you sure? 정말이야?

I'm in trouble. 큰일 났다.

Well, I will help you. 그래, 내가 도와줄께.

That's a good idea. 그거 좋은 생각이다.

Did you finish your homework?

Did you finish your homework?   Did you finish your homework?

Oops, I forgot it.

Oops, I forgot it.   Oops, I forgot it.

Are you sure?

Are you sure?   Are you sure?

I'm in trouble.

I'm in trouble.   I'm in trouble.

Well, I will help you.

Well, I will help you.   Well, I will help you.

That's a good idea.

That's a good idea.   That's a good idea.

4. 선생님

Good morning, sir.	안녕하세요, 선생님.
Good morning, everyone.	안녕, 여러분.
We respect you.	우리는 선생님을 존경합니다.
That sounds great.	근사하게 들리는구나.
We love you.	선생님을 사랑해요.
I love you, too.	나도 너희들을 사랑한다.

Good morning, sir.

Good morning, sir.　　　　Good morning, sir.

Good morning, everyone.

Good morning, everyone.　　Good morning, everyone.

We respect you.

We respect you.　　　　We respect you.

That sounds great.

That sounds great.　　　That sounds great.

We love you.

We love you.　　　　　We love you.

I love you, too.

I love you, too.　　　　I love you, too.

5. 질문

May I ask you a question? 질문 하나 해도 돼요?

Any question will do. 어떤 질문이든 해 봐.

Are you married? 결혼했어요?

No, not yet. 아니, 아직 못 했어.

That's good for you. 잘하신 일이에요.

What are you talking about? 무슨 말을 하는 거니?

May I ask you a question?

May I ask you a question?　　May I ask you a question?

Any question will do.

Any question will do.　　Any question will do.

Are you married?

Are you married?　　Are you married?

No, not yet.

No, not yet.　　No, not yet.

That's good for you.

That's good for you.　　That's good for you.

What are you talking about?

What are you talking about?　　What are you talking about?

6. 설명

Do you understand?	알겠어?
No, I don't understand.	모르겠는데요.
Is that so?	그래?
What does it mean?	그게 무슨 의미에요?
It's easy to understand.	이해하기 쉬운 것인데.
It might be true.	그럴지도 모르지요.

Do you understand?

Do you understand?　　　　Do you understand?

No, I don't understand.

No, I don't understand.　　　No, I don't understand.

Is that so?

Is that so?　　　　Is that so?

What does it mean?

What does it mean?　　　What does it mean?

It's easy to understand.

It's easy to understand.　　It's easy to understand.

It might be true.

It might be true　　　　It might be true

7. 의론

Let's talk about it.	그것에 대해 얘기해 보자.
What is the point?	요점이 뭐예요?
As you know, this is the point.	여러분이 알다시피, 이것이 요점이야.
Sure, it is.	네, 그렇군요.
Do you agree?	동의합니까?
Yes, I agree.	네, 동의합니다.

Let's talk about it.

Let's talk about it.
Let's talk about it.

What is the point?

What is the point?
What is the point?

As you know, this is the point.

As you know, this is the point.
As you know, this is the point.

Sure, it is.

Sure, it is.
Sure, it is.

Do you agree?

Do you agree?
Do you agree?

Yes, I agree.

Yes, I agree.
Yes, I agree.

1. 국어

Who will read these sentences? 누가 이 글을 읽어볼까요?

I will. 제가 읽겠어요.

Well done. 잘 했어요.

I hope so. 그러기를 바랍니다.

What do you think? 어떻게 생각해요?

I have no idea. 아무 생각 없어요.

Who will read these sentences?

Who will read these sentences?　　Who will read these sentences?

I will.

I will.　　I will.

Well done.

Well done.　　Well done.

I hope so.

I hope so.　　I hope so.

What do you think?

What do you think?　　What do you think?

I have no idea.

I have no idea.　　I have no idea.

2. 영어

My English is good enough.　　　내 영어는 괜찮은 편이지요.

Do you think so?　　　그렇게 생각해요?

Yes, I speak English very well.　　　네, 나는 영어를 아주 잘 합니다.

No, I don't think so.　　　아니요, 나는 그렇게 생각하지 않아요.

I beg your pardon.　　　다시 한 번 말해 주세요.

You make me laugh.　　　나를 웃기는군요.

My English is good enough.

My English is good enough.   My English is good enough.

Do you think so?

Do you think so?   Do you think so?

Yes, I speak English very well.

Yes, I speak English very well.   Yes, I speak English very well.

No, I don't think so.

No, I don't think so.   No, I don't think so.

I beg your pardon.

I beg your pardon.   I beg your pardon.

You make me laugh.

You make me laugh.   You make me laugh.

3. 수학

Five and seven is twelve.   5 더하기 7은 12입니다.

That's right.   맞았습니다.

Four times six is twenty four.   4 곱하기 6은 24입니다.

What a surprise!   놀랍군요!

Ninety nine devide by nine is what?   99 나누기 9는 얼마입니까?

It's a little hard.   좀 어렵군요.

$$3 \times 4 = 12$$
$$4 \times 4 = 16$$
$$5 \times 4 = 20$$
$$6 \times 4 = 24$$

Five and seven is twelve.

Five and seven is twelve.   Five and seven is twelve.

That's right.

That's right.   That's right.

Four times six is twenty four.

Four times six is twenty four.   Four times six is twenty four.

What a surprise!

What a surprise!   What a surprise!

Ninety nine devide by nine is what?

Ninety nine devide by nine is what?   Ninety nine devide by nine is what?

It's a little hard.

It's a little hard.   It's a little hard.

4. 사회

What is society?	사회란 무엇입니까?
Who knows?	누가 알겠습니까?
Who can tell me about that?	누가 말해 줄 수 있나요?
We can not make an answer.	우리는 답을 몰라요.
You must study it.	너희들 공부 좀 해야겠네요.
It would be better.	그것이 좋겠어요.

What is society?

What is society?

What is society?

Who knows?

Who knows?

Who knows?

Who can tell me about that?

Who can tell me about that?

Who can tell me about that?

We can not make an answer.

We can not make an answer.

We can not make an answer.

You must study it.

You must study it.

You must study it.

It would be better.

It would be better.

It would be better.

5. 과학

What is science? 과학이란 무엇입니까?

I know. 저는 압니다.

Where is the end of space? 우주의 끝은 어디입니까?

Nobody knows. 아무도 모릅니다.

How old is the earth? 지구는 얼마나 오래 되었나요?

It's not an important matter. 그것은 중요한 문제가 아닙니다.

What is science?

What is science?　　　　　　What is science?

I know.

I know.　　　　　　I know.

Where is the end of space?

Where is the end of space?　　Where is the end of space?

Nobody knows.

Nobody knows.　　　　　Nobody knows.

How old is the earth?

How old is the earth?　　　How old is the earth?

It's not an important matter.

It's not an important matter.　It's not an important matter.

6. 숙제

Here is homework for you.	숙제가 있습니다.
Good grief!	이럴 수가!
Calm down.	조용히 해요.
Let me go.	그냥 가게 해 주세요.
Don't forget it.	숙제 잊지 말아요.
I really don't want it.	나는 정말 원하지 않아요.

Here is homework for you.

Here is homework for you.   Here is homework for you.

Good grief!

Good grief!   Good grief!

Calm down.

Calm down.   Calm down.

Let me go.

Let me go.   Let me go.

Don't forget it.

Don't forget it.   Don't forget it.

I really don't want it.

I really don't want it.   I really don't want it.

7. 하교

Bye.	잘 가요.
Goodbye, sir.	안녕히 계세요, 선생님.
Have a nice day.	좋은 하루 되세요.
See you tomorrow, sir.	내일 뵙겠습니다, 선생님.
See you.	또 만나요.
Wow, now we are free.	야, 이제 우리는 자유다.

Bye.
Bye.

Bye.

Goodbye, sir.
Goodbye, sir.

Goodbye, sir.

Have a nice day.
Have a nice day.

Have a nice day.

See you tomorrow, sir.
See you tomorrow, sir.

See you tomorrow, sir.

See you.
See you.

See you.

Wow, now we are free.
Wow, now we are free.

Wow, now we are free.

1. 건강

What's wrong with you?	어디 불편해?
I feel sick.	아픈 것 같아요.
Are you alright?	괜찮아?
I got a bad cold.	감기에 걸렸어요.
Are you okay?	괜찮아?
Yes, I feel better.	네, 좀 나아진 것 같아요.

What's wrong with you?

What's wrong with you?

What's wrong with you?

I feel sick.

I feel sick.

I feel sick.

Are you alright?

Are you alright?

Are you alright?

I got a bad cold.

I got a bad cold.

I got a bad cold.

Are you okay?

Are you okay?

Are you okay?

Yes, I feel better.

Yes, I feel better.

Yes, I feel better.

2. 놀이

Let's play hide and sick.	숨바꼭질하자.
It will be fun.	그거 재미있겠다.
Scissor-rock-paper.	가위-바위-보.
It's your turn.	네 차례야.
After you.	너 먼저 해.
It's my turn.	내 차례야.

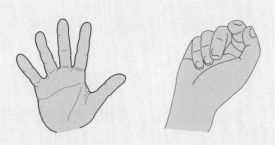

Let's play hide and sick.

Let's play hide and sick.　　　　Let's play hide and sick.

It will be fun.

It will be fun.　　　　It will be fun.

Scissor-rock-paper.

Scissor-rock-paper.　　　　Scissor-rock-paper.

It's your turn.

It's your turn.　　　　It's your turn.

After you.

After you.　　　　After you.

It's my turn.

It's my turn.　　　　It's my turn.

3. 체육

Ready, set, go.	준비, 차려, 출발.
No, stop.	아니, 멈추어요.
What's the matter?	무슨 일이야?
I give up.	포기할래요.
Do your best.	최선을 다 해.
I'm hurt.	다쳤어요.

Ready, set, go.

Ready, set, go.　　　　　　Ready, set, go.

No, stop.

No, stop.　　　　　　No, stop.

What's the matter?

What's the matter?　　　　　　What's the matter?

I give up.

I give up.　　　　　　I give up.

Do your best.

Do your best.　　　　　　Do your best.

I'm hurt.

I'm hurt.　　　　　　I'm hurt.

4. 음악

Listen to the music.	저 음악을 들어봐.
It's unbelievable.	믿을 수가 없어요.
Play it by yourself.	너도 한 번 해봐.
It's not easy.	쉽지 않아요.
How did you do?	어땠어?
Not bad.	나쁘지는 않았어요.

Listen to the music.

Listen to the music.　　　　　　Listen to the music.

It's unbelievable.

It's unbelievable.　　　　　　It's unbelievable.

Play it by yourself.

Play it by yourself.　　　　　　Play it by yourself.

It's not easy.

It's not easy.　　　　　　It's not easy.

How did you do?

How did you do?　　　　　　How did you do?

Not bad.

Not bad.　　　　　　Not bad.

5. 미술

May I have a look?	좀 봐도 될까요?
Why not?	왜 안 되겠어?
It looks great.	훌륭해 보이네요.
It's nothing.	별 거 아니야.
Look at my drawing.	제 그림 좀 봐주세요.
Way to go.	제대로 그렸네.

May I have a look?

May I have a look?   May I have a look?

Why not?

Why not?   Why not?

It looks great.

It looks great.   It looks great.

It's nothing.

It's nothing.   It's nothing.

Look at my drawing.

Look at my drawing.   Look at my drawing.

Way to go.

Way to go.   Way to go.

6. 실습

Let me try.	한 번 해보겠어요.
You can do it.	너는 할 수 있어.
I trust myself.	저는 저 자신을 믿습니다.
It makes sense.	일리 있는 말이다.
Here I am.	저는 합니다.
May you succeed!	성공을 기원하겠어!

Let me try.

Let me try.　　　　　　　　Let me try.

You can do it.

You can do it.　　　　　　You can do it.

I trust myself.

I trust myself.　　　　　　I trust myself.

It makes sense.

It makes sense.　　　　　　It makes sense.

Here I am.

Here I am.　　　　　　　Here I am.

May you succeed!

May you succeed!　　　　May you succeed!

7. 결과

How was it?	어땠어요?
It was pretty good.	상당히 좋았어.
Is that all?	그게 전부에요?
Wait a minute, please.	그런데, 잠깐만.
Is there any problem?	무슨 문제라도 있나요?
No problem.	아니, 문제없어.

How was it?

How was it?　　　　　　　　　　How was it?

It was pretty good.

It was pretty good.　　　　　It was pretty good.

Is that all?

Is that all?　　　　　　　　　Is that all?

Wait a minute, please.

Wait a minute, please.　　　Wait a minute, please.

Is there any problem?

Is there any problem?　　　Is there any problem?

No problem.

No problem.　　　　　　　　No problem.

1. 전화

Hello, this is Dante speaking.	여보세요, 단테입니다.
Hello, this is Einstein.	여보세요, 아인쉬타인입니다.
May I speak to Mr. Da Vinci?	다 빈치씨와 통화할 수 있을까요?
Hold on, please.	잠깐만 기다리세요.
Da Vinci is speaking.	다 빈치입니다.
Hello, how are you.	네, 안녕하세요.

Hello, this is Dante speaking.

Hello, this is Dante speaking. Hello, this is Dante speaking.

Hello, this is Einstein.

Hello, this is Einstein. Hello, this is Einstein.

May I speak to Mr. Da Vinci?

May I speak to Mr. Da Vinci? May I speak to Mr. Da Vinci?

Hold on, please.

Hold on, please. Hold on, please.

Da Vinci is speaking.

Da Vinci is speaking. Da Vinci is speaking.

Hello, how are you.

Hello, how are you. Hello, how are you.

2. 예약

May I make an appointment?	약속을 좀 할 수 있을까요?
Of course.	물론입니다.
I want to visit your office.	선생님 사무실을 방문하고 싶습니다.
Any time you want.	언제든지 좋은 때 오십시요.
It's very kind of you.	아주 친절하시군요.
Thank you for calling.	전화해 줘서 고맙습니다.

May I make an appointment?

May I make an appointment? May I make an appointment?

Of course.

Of course. Of course.

I want to visit your office.

I want to visit your office. I want to visit your office.

Any time you want.

Any time you want. Any time you want.

It's very kind of you.

It's very kind of you. It's very kind of you.

Thank you for calling.

Thank you for calling. Thank you for calling.

3. 사무실

May I come in?	들어가도 좋습니까?
Please, come in.	네, 어서 들어 오십시요.
May I have a seat?	앉아도 될까요?
Make yourself at home.	집처럼 편하게 하세요.
We don't want to be any bother.	우리는 방해가 되고 싶지 않습니다.
No, not at all.	아니요, 천만에요.

May I come in?

May I come in? May I come in?

Please, come in.

Please, come in. Please, come in.

May I have a seat?

May I have a seat? May I have a seat?

Make yourself at home.

Make yourself at home. Make yourself at home.

We don't want to be any bother.

We don't want to be any bother. We don't want to be any bother.

No, not at all.

No, not at all. No, not at all.

4. 공장

You must keep the rules.   규칙을 지켜야 합니다.

I see.   알겠습니다.

Please go ahead.   들어가 보세요.

What's going on?   무슨 일 있습니까?

Watch your step.   발걸음을 조심하세요.

Don't worry.   걱정 마십시오.

You must keep the rules.

You must keep the rules.　　　　You must keep the rules.

I see.

I see.　　　　I see.

Please go ahead.

Please go ahead.　　　　Please go ahead.

What's going on?

What's going on?　　　　What's going on?

Watch your step.

Watch your step.　　　　Watch your step.

Don't worry.

Don't worry.　　　　Don't worry.

5. 휴게실

I want to take a rest.	잠깐 쉬고 싶습니다.
Let's have a break.	휴식시간을 가집시다.
I had so much to learn.	배울 것이 아주 많았어요.
That would be great.	그렇다면 대단히 좋은 일이지요.
Thank you for your kindness.	친절에 감사드립니다.
You're welcome.	천만에요.

I want to take a rest.
I want to take a rest. I want to take a rest.

Let's have a break.
Let's have a break. Let's have a break.

I had so much to learn.
I had so much to learn. I had so much to learn.

That would be great.
That would be great. That would be great.

Thank you for your kindness.
Thank you for your kindness. Thank you for your kindness.

You're welcome.
You're welcome. You're welcome.

6. 시장

What are you looking for?	무엇을 찾고 계십니까?
How much is this?	이것은 얼마입니까?
It has a good price.	그것은 값이 적당합니다.
That's cheap.	싸군요.
Which is better?	어느 것이 더 좋습니까?
I want both of them.	둘 다 갖고 싶습니다.

What are you looking for?

What are you looking for?　　　What are you looking for?

How much is this?

How much is this?　　　How much is this?

It has a good price.

It has a good price.　　　It has a good price.

That's cheap.

That's cheap.　　　That's cheap.

Which is better?

Which is better?　　　Which is better?

I want both of them.

I want both of them.　　　I want both of them.

7. 백화점

What a crowd!	사람 많네!
How about this one?	이것은 어떻습니까?
It's expensive.	좀 비싸네요.
May I show you cheaper one?	싼 것을 보여드릴까요?
Could you give me a discount?	값을 좀 깎아주실 수 있습니까?
I'm sorry.	죄송합니다.

What a crowd!

What a crowd! | What a crowd!

How about this one?

How about this one? | How about this one?

It's expensive.

It's expensive. | It's expensive.

May I show you cheaper one?

May I show you cheaper one? | May I show you cheaper one?

Could you give me a discount?

Could you give me a discount? | Could you give me a discount?

I'm sorry.

I'm sorry. | I'm sorry.

1. 시간

What date is it today?	오늘 며칠이야?
It's June 23rd.	6월 23일이야.
What day is it today?	오늘 무슨 요일이야?
It's Thursday.	목요일이야.
What time is it now?	지금 몇 시야?
It's half past three.	세시 반이야.

What date is it today?

What date is it today?   What date is it today?

It's June 23rd.

It's June 23rd.   It's June 23rd.

What day is it today?

What day is it today?   What day is it today?

It's Thursday.

It's Thursday.   It's Thursday.

What time is it now?

What time is it now?   What time is it now?

It's half past three.

It's half past three.   It's half past three.

2. 약속

Do you have time tomorrow afternoon?　　내일 오후에 시간 있어?

Let me check.　　어디 보자.

Shall we meet tomorrow?　　내일 만날 수 있을까?

I will wait for you.　　너를 기다리고 있겠어.

I will be there at 3 o'clock.　　세시에 그곳에 가겠어.

OK, see you then.　　좋아, 그때 만나자.

Do you have time tomorrow afternoon?

Do you have time tomorrow afternoon?   Do you have time tomorrow afternoon?

Let me check.

Let me check.   Let me check.

Shall we meet tomorrow?

Shall we meet tomorrow?   Shall we meet tomorrow?

I will wait for you.

I will wait for you.   I will wait for you.

I will be there at 3 o'clock.

I will be there at 3 o'clock.   I will be there at 3 o'clock.

OK, see you then.

OK, see you then.   OK, see you then.

3. 장소

Where to?	어디 가?
I'm going to the meeting place.	약속 장소로 가고 있어.
Is it far?	멀어?
No, it's not so far.	아니, 아주 멀지는 않아.
How long will it take?	얼마나 걸려?
It takes about 20 minutes.	약 20분 정도 걸리지.

Where to?

Where to?   Where to?

I'm going to the meeting place.

I'm going to the meeting place.   I'm going to the meeting place.

Is it far?

Is it far?   Is it far?

No, it's not so far.

No, it's not so far.   No, it's not so far.

How long will it take?

How long will it take?   How long will it take?

It takes about 20 minutes.

It takes about 20 minutes.   It takes about 20 minutes.

4. 만남

How are you?	잘 있었니?
Fine, thank you. And you?	그래, 잘 있었어. 너는 어때?
Long time no see.	오랫동안 못 보았었지.
I'm happy to see you again.	너를 다시 만나서 기쁘구나.
You look good.	좋아 보인다.
How have you been?	그 동안 어떻게 지냈니?

How are you?

How are you?　　　　　　How are you?

Fine, thank you. And you?

Fine, thank you. And you?　　Fine, thank you. And you?

Long time no see.

Long time no see.　　　　Long time no see.

I'm happy to see you again.

I'm happy to see you again.　　I'm happy to see you again.

You look good.

You look good.　　　　　You look good.

How have you been?

How have you been?　　　How have you been?

5. 소개

May I introduce my friend?	내 친구를 소개해도 될까?
Of course, you do.	물론, 그렇게 해야지.
This is my friend David.	여기는 내 친구 데이빗이야.
Nice to meet you. I'm Kate.	만나서 반가워. 나 케이트야.
Glad to see you, Kate.	만나서 반가워, 케이트.
Come on, let's have a seat.	자, 자리에 앉자.

May I introduce my friend?

May I introduce my friend?   May I introduce my friend?

Of course, you do.

Of course, you do.   Of course, you do.

This is my friend David.

This is my friend David.   This is my friend David.

Nice to meet you. I'm Kate.

Nice to meet you. I'm Kate.   Nice to meet you. I'm Kate.

Glad to see you, Kate.

Glad to see you, Kate.   Glad to see you, Kate.

Come on, let's have a seat.

Come on, let's have a seat.   Come on, let's have a seat.

6. 대화

Where are you from?	어느 나라에서 왔니?
I'm from Australia.	호주에서 왔어.
Where do you live?	어디에 사니?
I live in Seoul.	서울에서 살고 있어.
How long have you been in Korea?	한국에 온 지 얼마나 되었어?
Almost two and a half years.	거의 2년 반 되었어.

Where are you from?

Where are you from?　　　　Where are you from?

I'm from Australia.

I'm from Australia.　　　　I'm from Australia.

Where do you live?

Where do you live?　　　　Where do you live?

I live in Seoul.

I live in Seoul.　　　　I live in Seoul.

How long have you been in Korea?

How long have you been in Korea?　　How long have you been in Korea?

Almost two and a half years.

Almost two and a half years.　　Almost two and a half years.

7. 작별

I have to go.	가야겠어.
So soon?	그렇게 빨리?
May I see you again?	다시 만날 수 있을까?
Whenever you want.	원하면 언제든지.
The sooner, the better.	빠르면 빠를수록 좋겠다.
Likewise!	나도 그래!

I have to go.

I have to go.   I have to go.

So soon?

So soon?   So soon?

May I see you again?

May I see you again?   May I see you again?

Whenever you want.

Whenever you want.   Whenever you want.

The sooner, the better.

The sooner, the better.   The sooner, the better.

Likewise!

Likewise!   Likewise!

제 36 일

1. 잔치

When is your birthday?	네 생일이 언제지?
It's my birthday today.	오늘이 내 생일이야.
Congratulations, happy birthday!	생일 축하해!
We are having a party tonight.	오늘밤에 잔치가 있어.
That's fantastic.	그거 멋있구나.
Come and enjoy yourself!	와서 즐겁게 놀아.

When is your birthday?

When is your birthday?　　　　When is your birthday?

It's my birthday today.

It's my birthday today.　　　　It's my birthday today.

Congratulations, happy birthday!

Congratulations, happy birthday!　　Congratulations, happy birthday!

We are having a party tonight.

We are having a party tonight.　　We are having a party tonight.

That's fantastic.

That's fantastic.　　　　That's fantastic.

Come and enjoy yourself!

Come and enjoy yourself!　　　　Come and enjoy yourself!

2. 선물

This is for you.	너에게 주는 거야.
You make me happy.	너는 나를 행복하게 하는구나.
How do you like it?	그거 어때?
I love it very much.	아주 마음에 들어.
We are proud of you.	우리는 너를 자랑스럽게 생각해.
I'm really happy.	나는 정말 행복해.

This is for you.

This is for you.   This is for you.

You make me happy.

You make me happy.   You make me happy.

How do you like it?

How do you like it?   How do you like it?

I love it very much.

I love it very much.   I love it very much.

We are proud of you.

We are proud of you.   We are proud of you.

I'm really happy.

I'm really happy.   I'm really happy.

3. 음식

I'm very hungry.	배가 너무 고프다.
Help yourself!	갖다 먹어.
I have got it.	알았어.
Don't eat too much!	너무 많이 먹지 마!
Never mind.	신경 쓰지 마.
Is it so good?	그렇게 맛있니?

I'm very hungry.

I'm very hungry.   I'm very hungry.

Help yourself!

Help yourself!   Help yourself!

I have got it.

I have got it.   I have got it.

Don't eat too much!

Don't eat too much!   Don't eat too much!

Never mind.

Never mind.   Never mind.

Is it so good?

Is it so good?   Is it so good?

4. 오락

Let's play games.	놀이하자.
That's what I want.	그건 내가 바라던 바야.
What games?	어떤 놀이?
I don't care.	아무래도 좋아.
How is this?	이건 어때?
It doesn't matter.	상관없어.

Let's play games.

Let's play games.　　　　　　Let's play games.

That's what I want.

That's what I want.　　　　　That's what I want.

What games?

What games?　　　　　　　What games?

I don't care.

I don't care.　　　　　　　I don't care.

How is this?

How is this?　　　　　　　How is this?

It doesn't matter.

It doesn't matter.　　　　　It doesn't matter.

5. 소식

Listen to me.	내 얘기 들어봐.
What's up?	무슨 일 있어?
Here is the news.	뉴스가 있어.
That's a lie.	그거 거짓말이다.
No kidding!	농담하지 마!
I'm shocked.	난 충격 받았다.

Listen to me.
Listen to me.　　　　　Listen to me.

What's up?
What's up?　　　　　What's up?

Here is the news.
Here is the news.　　　　　Here is the news.

That's a lie.
That's a lie.　　　　　That's a lie.

No kidding!
No kidding!　　　　　No kidding!

I'm shocked.
I'm shocked.　　　　　I'm shocked.

6. 소란

Don't make fun of me.	나를 놀리지 마.
Shame on you!	부끄러운 줄 알아라!
I can't stand it.	나는 참을 수가 없어.
Who cares?	누가 어쨌다고?
So what?	그래서 뭐?
Hold it!	그만 해!

Don't make fun of me.

Don't make fun of me.

Don't make fun of me.

Shame on you!

Shame on you!

Shame on you!

I can't stand it.

I can't stand it.

I can't stand it.

Who cares?

Who cares?

Who cares?

So what?

So what?

So what?

Hold it!

Hold it!

Hold it!

7. 기분

I feel good.	기분 좋구나.
I feel bad.	기분 나쁘다.
I'm surprised.	놀랐다.
I'm shy.	부끄럽구나.
I'm just so so.	난 그저 그래.
Leave me alone.	나 혼자 있게 내버려 둬.

I feel good.

I feel good.   I feel good.

I feel bad.

I feel bad.   I feel bad.

I'm surprised.

I'm surprised.   I'm surprised.

I'm shy.

I'm shy.   I'm shy.

I'm just so so.

I'm just so so.   I'm just so so.

Leave me alone.

Leave me alone.   Leave me alone.

1. 날씨

It's a nice day.	상쾌한 날이군요.
It's fine day today.	오늘 날씨가 정말 좋습니다.
Clouds are coming.	구름이 몰려오네요.
It's raining.	비가 오네요.
Oh, my!	아니, 이런!
The sun is shining again.	해가 다시 비추네요.

It's a nice day.

It's a nice day.　　　　　　　It's a nice day.

It's fine day today.

It's fine day today.　　　　　It's fine day today.

Clouds are coming.

Clouds are coming.　　　　　Clouds are coming.

It's raining.

It's raining.　　　　　　　　It's raining.

Oh, my!

Oh, my!　　　　　　　　　　Oh, my!

The sun is shining again.

The sun is shining again.　　The sun is shining again.

2. 출발

Are you ready?	준비 됐나요?
Yes, I am ready.	네, 준비 됐어요.
Is there anything else?	더 필요한 것이 있나요?
That's enough.	다 되었어요.
Let's get going.	자, 떠납시다.
Shall we go?	갈까요?

Are you ready?

Are you ready?　　　　　Are you ready?

Yes, I am ready.

Yes, I am ready.　　　　Yes, I am ready.

Is there anything else?

Is there anything else?　　Is there anything else?

That's enough.

That's enough.　　　　That's enough.

Let's get going.

Let's get going.　　　　Let's get going.

Shall we go?

Shall we go?　　　　Shall we go?

3. 산

What a mountain!	산이여!
Watch out!	조심해!
What should I do?	어떻게 해야 됩니까?
Do as I do.	나하는 대로 해.
Like this?	이렇게요?
That's the way.	그래 그거야.

What a mountain!

What a mountain!   What a mountain!

Watch out!

Watch out!   Watch out!

What should I do?

What should I do?   What should I do?

Do as I do.

Do as I do.   Do as I do.

Like this?

Like this?   Like this?

That's the way.

That's the way.   That's the way.

4. 바다

Look at the endless waves.	저 끝없는 파도를 봐.
I do.	보고 있어.
I hear the songs of the sea.	나는 바다의 노래를 듣고 있어.
Me, too.	나도.
Why is the sea water salty?	바닷물은 왜 짜지?
We never know.	우리는 모르지.

Look at the endless waves.

Look at the endless waves.　　　Look at the endless waves.

I do.

I do.　　　I do.

I hear the songs of the sea.

I hear the songs of the sea.　　　I hear the songs of the sea.

Me, too.

Me, too.　　　Me, too.

Why is the sea water salty?

Why is the sea water salty?　　　Why is the sea water salty?

We never know.

We never know.　　　We never know.

5. 하늘

The sky is really blue.	하늘이 정말 푸르구나.
That's it.	그건 그래.
I want to be a cloud.	나는 한 조각 구름이 되고 싶어.
It's up to you.	네 마음대로 해.
Let's fly like a bird.	새처럼 날아보자.
What for?	뭣 때문에?

The sky is really blue.

The sky is really blue.   The sky is really blue.

That's it.

That's it.   That's it.

I want to be a cloud.

I want to be a cloud.   I want to be a cloud.

It's up to you.

It's up to you.   It's up to you.

Let's fly like a bird.

Let's fly like a bird.   Let's fly like a bird.

What for?

What for?   What for?

6. 마음

What is nature?	자연이란 무엇인가요?
It's a matter of opinion.	그것은 생각의 문제에요.
Who preserve nature?	누가 자연을 지키나요?
It's me.	접니다.
Yes, it's you.	그래, 네가 해야지.
I will take care of it.	내가 보살펴 줄 겁니다.

What is nature?

What is nature?　　　　　What is nature?

It's a matter of opinion.

It's a matter of opinion.　　　It's a matter of opinion.

Who preserve nature?

Who preserve nature?　　　Who preserve nature?

It's me.

It's me.　　　　　　　It's me.

Yes, it's you.

Yes, it's you.　　　　　Yes, it's you.

I will take care of it.

I will take care of it.　　　I will take care of it.

7. 귀가

I'm home.	다녀왔습니다.
Are you tired?	피곤하니?
There's no place like home.	집처럼 좋은 곳은 없어요.
It's time to go to sleep.	이제 잘 시간이야.
Good night.	안녕히 주무세요.
Have a good dream.	좋은 꿈 꾸어라.

I'm home.

I'm home.

I'm home.

Are you tired?

Are you tired?

Are you tired?

There's no place like home.

There's no place like home.

There's no place like home.

It's time to go to sleep.

It's time to go to sleep.

It's time to go to sleep.

Good night.

Good night.

Good night.

Have a good dream.

Have a good dream.

Have a good dream.

✳ 아래의 문장을 영어는 한글로, 한글은 영어로 옮기십시오. 제한시간은 20분입니다.

1 It's time to get up.

➡ --

2 Well, I will help you.

➡ --

3 Any question will do.

➡ --

4 Yes, I agree.

➡ --

5 It's your turn.

➡ --

6 Make yourself at home

➡ --

7 I will wait for you.

➡ --

8 How long will it take?

➡ --

9 Where do you live?

➡ --

10 We are proud of you.

➡ --

점 수

11 I don't care.

➡ --

12 Shame on you!

➡ --

13 Leave me alone.

➡ --

14 It's up to you.

➡ --

15 Have a good dream.

➡ --

16 뭐하고 있어?

➡ --

17 전화해 줘서 고맙습니다.

➡ --

18 어느 것이 더 좋습니까?

➡ --

19 너무 많이 먹지 마!

➡ --

20 준비 됐나요?

➡ --

A

B

C

D

F

G

H

Y

최 종 수

서울에서 출생하였으며, 연세대학교 국문학과를 졸업하였습니다. 연세대학교 한국어학당에서 한국어 강사를 지냈고, 현재 도서출판 역민사 대표로 있습니다. 저서로는 〈비 해피 영어단어〉(초등학교 3학년~6학년, 전 16권), 〈비 해피 영어문법〉, 〈WQ·EQ·IQ 테스트〉, 〈가을빛에 지다〉, 〈세계사 연대기〉(공동편저) 등이 있습니다.

비 해피 영어회화

- 초등학생 영어회화 -

2005년 7월 25일 초판 1쇄 발행

엮은이 최종수
편집 강면실
디자인 조승현
마케팅 김인호
만든곳 YMS미디어

등록 2004. 1. 10. 서울 제 2-3912호
주소 100-013 서울 중구 충무로 3가 59-23
전화 2274-9411
팩스 2268-3619
e-mail ymsbp@yahoo.co.kr

ISBN 89-91077-23-4 63740

값 5,000원

이 책을 다 공부한 학생들은 자신의 영어실력 향상에
놀라움을 감추지 못하고 있습니다.

비 해피 영어문법

최종수 엮음

전국의 유명서점에서도 이 책의 출현을 반가워하고 있습니다.

- 문법의 이해는 영어를 잘 하기 위한 최선의 길입니다.

- 여기의 예문은 쓰면서 익히도록 되어 있습니다.

- 매일 두 페이지씩 공부합니다.

- 부모님들은 학습 결과를 바로 알 수 있습니다.

초등학교 고학년이면 누구나 혼자 할 수 있습니다.
부모님이 옆에서 봐주면 학습 효과가 더욱 높아집니다.

112쪽 5,000원

비 해피 영어 교육 센터 **YMS미디어**
전화 2274-9411 팩스 2268-3619

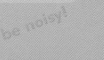

1 일어날 시간이야.

2 그래, 내가 도와줄께.

3 어떤 질문이든 해 봐.

4 네, 동의합니다.

5 네 차례야.

6 집처럼 편하게 하세요.

7 너를 기다리고 있겠어.

8 얼마나 걸려?

9 어디에 사니?

10 우리는 너를 자랑스럽게 생각해.

11 아무래도 좋아.

12 부끄러운 줄 알아라!

13 나 혼자 있게 내버려 둬.

14 네 마음대로 해.

15 좋은 꿈 꾸어라.

16 What are you doing?

17 Thank you for calling.

18 Which is better?

19 Don't eat too much!

20 Are you ready?